W9-CFC-572

MH-53E SEA DRAGONS

CRETE PUBLIC LIBRARY
N. MAIN
CRETE, IL 60417
708/672-8017

BY CARLOS ALVAREZ

BELLWETHER MEDIA · MINNEAPOLIS, MN

Are you ready to take it to the extreme?
Torque books thrust you into the action-packed
world of sports, vehicles, and adventure. These books
may include dirt, smoke, fire, and dangerous stunts.
WARNING: read at your own risk.

Library of Congress Cataloging-in-Publication Data

Alvarez, Carlos, 1968-
 MH-53E Sea Dragons / by Carlos Alvarez.
    p. cm. – (Torque: Military machines)
 Includes bibliographical references and index.
 Summary: "Amazing photography accompanies engaging information about MH-53E Sea Dragons. The
combination of high-interest subject matter and light text is intended for students in grades 3 through
7"–Provided by publisher.
 ISBN 978-1-60014-495-0 (hardcover : alk. paper)
 1. Sikorsky H-53 (Military transport helicopter)–Juvenile literature. 2. United States. Navy–Search and
rescue operations–Juvenile literature. I. Title.
 UG1232.T72A458 2010
 623.74'65–dc22   2010000864

This edition first published in 2011 by Bellwether Media, Inc.

No part of this publication may be reproduced in whole or in part without written permission of
the publisher. For information regarding permission, write to Bellwether Media, Inc., Attention:
Permissions Department, 5357 Penn Avenue South, Minneapolis, MN 55419.

Text copyright © 2011 by Bellwether Media, Inc. TORQUE and associated logos are trademarks and/or
registered trademarks of Bellwether Media, Inc.

The images in this book are reproduced through the courtesy of: Ted Carlson/Fotodynamics, pp. 7, 10-11,
13, 21; Agustin Anaya/Airliners, p. 20; all other photos courtesy of the Department of Defense.

Printed in the United States of America, North Mankato, MN.
080110   1162

J
623.74
ALV

3 1886 00174 6713

CONTENTS

THE MH-53E SEA DRAGON IN ACTION

The water is calm off the coast of an enemy country. However, the United States Navy knows that danger lurks beneath the surface. Enemy **mines** are hidden under the water. The mines are a threat to U.S. ships and their crews. An MH-53E Sea Dragon rises into the air.

The Sea Dragon crew uses sensors to find a minefield. They attach a device called a **countermeasure** to a cable. The Sea Dragon drags the countermeasure over the water toward the minefield.

countermeasure

★ **FAST FACT** ★

The Sea Dragon can travel at speeds up to 173 miles (278 kilometers) per hour.

7

A spray of water shoots into the air. The countermeasure has set off a mine. More explosions follow. The Sea Dragon crew keeps looking for mines. They won't stop until the area is safe for the Navy ships.

AIRBORNE MINE COUNTERMEASURES

The sea near enemy territory can be dangerous. Enemies can set up mines to destroy ships. The Navy needs ships and aircraft with countermeasures to search for and destroy these mines. This is the job of the MH-53E Sea Dragon.

The Sea Dragon is capable of transporting up to 55 troops.

BLACKHAWKS

16

The Sea Dragon entered Navy service in 1981. The Navy used the CH-53E Super Stallion as the model for the Sea Dragon. The Super Stallion is a large cargo helicopter. The Navy added mine-detecting gear to the Sea Dragon. It also added larger fuel tanks. These additions made the MH-53E the largest helicopter in the U.S. military.

Super Stallion

WEAPONS AND FEATURES

The Sea Dragon has many sensor systems to find mines. The **AN/AQS-20 Sonar Detecting Set** uses sound waves to detect mines. Sea Dragon crews also use the **Airborne Laser Mine Detection System**. This system uses **lasers** to find mines in shallow water.

.50-caliber machine gun

The Sea Dragon has mounts for .50-caliber machine guns. It carries no other weapons.

Mk 105

The crew uses countermeasures to
destroy mines. Many of these systems
are towed behind the Sea Dragon.
The Mk 105 is a minesweeping sled.
The Sea Dragon pulls the Mk 105
through an area that has mines.
The Mk 105's powerful magnets
set off the mines. The crew can
also use **acoustic** countermeasures.
These devices use sound waves to
set off mines.

<u>MH-53E SEA DRAGON</u>
<u>SPECIFICATIONS:</u>

Primary Function: Airborne mine
countermeasures

Length: 73 feet, 4 inches (22.4 meters)

Height: 28 feet, 4 inches (8.6 meters)

Rotor Diameter: 79 feet (24.1 meters)

Maximum Weight: 69,750 pounds
(31,640 kilograms)

Top Speed: 173 miles (278 kilometers)
per hour

Ceiling: 10,000 feet (3,048 meters)

Range: 1,208 miles (1,944 kilometers)

Crew: 3 or more

MH-53E MISSIONS

The Sea Dragon's main **mission** is to clear mines. The crew uses sensors to find underwater mines. Then they must decide which countermeasures to use to destroy those mines. The Sea Dragon can also perform **secondary** missions. It can deliver cargo to ships and even provide support in an attack.

19

The MH-53E has a crew of at least three. Two pilots work together to fly the helicopter. One or more crew members operate the helicopter's countermeasures. Every detected mine must be destroyed. Sailors depend on the Sea Dragon and its crew to keep their ships safe.

GLOSSARY

acoustic—using sound waves

Airborne Laser Mine Detection System—the equipment aboard a Sea Dragon that uses laser beams to detect mines in shallow water

AN/AQS-20 Sonar Detecting Set—the equipment aboard a Sea Dragon that uses sound waves to detect mines

countermeasure—a device used to safely detonate an explosive

lasers—highly focused beams of light

mines—hidden explosives that go off when a person, vehicle, or ship touches or gets near them

mission—a military task

secondary—less important

TO LEARN MORE

AT THE LIBRARY

Axelrod, Alan. *The Encyclopedia of the U.S. Navy*. New York, N.Y.: Checkmark Books, 2006.

David, Jack. *United States Navy*. Minneapolis, Minn.: Bellwether Media, 2008.

Hamilton, John. *The Navy*. Edina, Minn.: ABDO Publishing, 2007.

ON THE WEB

Learning more about military machines is as easy as 1, 2, 3.

1. Go to www.factsurfer.com.

2. Enter "military machines" into the search box.

3. Click the "Surf" button and you will see a list of related Web sites.

With factsurfer.com, finding more information is just a click away.

INDEX